BRITISH INDEPENDENT
BUS COMPANIES
SINCE THE 1970s

JOHN LAW

FONTHILL

The early days of independent buses are illustrated by this photo of a Vulcan saloon owned by Blue Ensign (Ennifer) of Doncaster, seen at its Waterdale stance.

A classic line up of independent buses in Doncaster. Reliance of Stainforth owned Guy Arab EJW456 is closest to the camera at the Christchurch terminus.

First published 2012

Fonthill Media Limited
www.fonthillmedia.com

Copyright © John Law 2012

John Law has asserted his rights under the Copyright, Designs and Patents Act 1988 to be identified as the Author of this work.

ISBN 978-1-78155-063-2 (PRINT)
ISBN 978-1-78155-139-4 (E-BOOK)

A CIP catalogue record for this book is available from the British Library.

Typeset in 9.5pt on 12pt Mrs Eaves Serif Narrow.
Typesetting by Fonthill Media. Printed in the UK.

connect with us
 facebook.com/fonthillmedia twitter.com/fonthillmedia

Introduction

I first became interested in buses during my early teens, when I was introduced to the hobby by schoolfriends Don Penney and Dave Ingram. Their influence led me to join the local 'Bus Club', the Doncaster Omnibus & Light Railway Society, where I learnt about the bus scene in the UK and beyond. However, even in those formative years, I became fascinated by the independent bus operators of the 'Donny' area, of which there were many.

My later teenage years were spent chasing beer and loose women, like many a lad of that age, so it was not until around 1973 that I regained my involvement in the world of omnibuses. Since then, I've been photographing the operations of the bus companies of Great Britain and now have a vast collection of images to bring to the fore.

While many enthusiasts have concentrated their efforts on photographing the major bus concerns, I have never forgotten those little companies like Leon, Blue Line, Rossie Motors and United Services running into Doncaster. Other British towns like Colchester, Paisley and Cannock were also famous for their independent operators.

So, what is an independent operator? To answer that question, we must delve back into history, when bus services were in their infancy. It was often the case that the local farmer converted his lorry to passenger carrying duties on market days. Demand grew and operations expanded, with purpose-built vehicles being obtained. Gradually, larger companies were formed from the merger or buy-out of the smaller ones. In turn, these became part of the big concerns, a metamorphosis still taking place today.

The introduction of the Road Traffic Act in 1930 brought regulation to the bus industry and this, in turn, brought about the demise of many small bus companies. The capital, in particular, lost many independents to the power of the London Transport Board. Elsewhere, the railways increased their involvement in the bus industry, while municipalities often prevented further independent expansion of competing services in their areas.

By the 1960s, there were two massive companies in England, the Tilling Group (owned by the nationalised British Transport Commission) and the British Electric Traction Company, while the Scottish Bus Group performed similar duties north of the border. Virtually all public transport in Northern Ireland had been nationalised. Outside of the conglomerates were a number of municipal operators and a host of independents. These ranged from large businesses like West Riding and Lancashire United to the one-bus operations of Chaloner's of Wrexham.

By 1969, the BET and BTC groups had combined to form the National Bus Company, while a short time later, the Passenger Transport Executives swallowed up municipal operators in the major conurbations. Both the NBC and the PTEs continued to expand by taking over the local independents.

A massive change to the bus industry occurred in 1986, when the Conservative Government of the time brought about deregulation. Suddenly, anyone with a bus was able to obtain a license to run a stage carriage service. Independent bus operators sprang up everywhere, even in the most unlikely of places.

GWR318, a Leyland Tiger of Pennine Motor Services, Gargrave, is waiting to head home in Skipton bus station in the early 1960s.

Towns and cities with no recent history of independent bus operations, such as Bristol and Sevenoaks, became worthy of my frequent visits. Shares in Agfa and Kodak must have gone up, given the amount of film I was using! Meanwhile, the National Bus Company was being split up and sold off.

Since then, three major groups have appeared: First, Stagecoach, and Arriva. There are also several smaller concerns, such as the Go Ahead Group. All have expanded by buying out the operations of both independent companies and former municipalities. Nevertheless, there are still a goodly number of independent bus operators in these islands and long may they continue.

So, now I can answer that question, 'what is an independent operator?' – any business running buses on stage carriage services that was, or is, outside of any of the groups mentioned above. I have, within these pages, attempted to depict a good cross-section of Britain's independent buses. Inevitably, in a book of this size and nature, I cannot illustrate every single operator or vehicle type, so I apologise if your favourite is not included.

My thanks must go to all the bus companies and their employees for their co-operation in the production of this book, by allowing access to their depots, or slowing down their buses as I took my photos. Every bit of assistance is gratefully acknowledged. I must also thank the following for their help: Jim Sambrooks, Michael Penn, Paul Roberts, and Peter Tuffrey, plus the many website owners who have provided information via the internet.

John Law, Stevenage

We start our tour of the UK in the most northerly islands, the Shetlands. Until being taken over, Shalder Coaches ran many services on both Shetland and Orkney. Here, in June 1999, MAN/Marshall bus S88JPS arrives at Whiteness to pick up passengers for Lerwick. The passengers will be enjoying great views of the loch. Most former Shalder services are now operated by Stagecoach.

Once the Skye Bridge opened, Clan Coaches of Kyle of Lochalsh (trading as Skye-Ways) were able to operate bus services to the island's capital, Portree. A small fleet of AEC Reliance coaches was in regular use, but this was supplemented by a Mercedes O405 bus, bought new. Here it is, registered N4SKY, passing the Sligachan Hotel, in the shadow of the Cuilin Mountains on Skye. The year is 1998, prior to when the Sligachan Hotel started brewing its own beer.

Moving now to the Outer Hebrides, we come to Stornoway, the largest town on Lewis and Harris, attracting services from all corners of the island. At the tiny bus station are two Bedford SB5 buses, KJS555R and PJS10L, both bodied by Willowbrook. They are in the fleet of Lochs Motor Transport, one of many operators running this type of bus when this photograph was taken in 1982.

Upon my arrival in Stornoway in 1982, I was greeted by horizontal rain, but five minutes later, the sun came out and I was able to photograph this former United Counties Ford R1014/Duple Dominant bus resting by the quayside. OVV51R is in the fleet of MacIver's, based in Stornoway itself.

We've now arrived on the Scottish mainland in June 1979. The Sutherland Transport and Trading Company ran services through the remoter parts of northern Scotland. Here, HGA981D, a Bedford VAS1/Duple Midland bus fitted with mail compartment, meets the early morning trains at Lairg railway station, a true example of transport integration. ST&T ceased trading in the early 1980s.

A & C McLennan of Spittalfield, to the north of Perth, owned a fascinating fleet of buses, used on their stage services in the area. Here's a sunny view of the depot yard, with Ford Thames/ Burlingham coach 67CVD, in May 1977. The Stagecoach Group now run most of the area's bus routes.

The area to the north and east of Dundee was mainly served by Northern Scottish, but the monopoly was broken by a few independents. One of these was Greyhound of Arbroath, who owned GNU266C, an ex-Chesterfield Corporation Daimler CCG6 with Weymann body, seen here in the snow at its Dundee terminus in early 1980. Greyhound was unusual in that there was also a depot in Sheffield, from where several steelworks contracts were operated.

After 1986, in common with the rest of mainland Britain, many coach businesses expanded into stage carriage work. Fife operator Moffat & Williamson took advantage of deregulation with routes throughout the Kingdom and over the Tay into Dundee. It is here, in the summer of 1993, that I photographed GMS280S. This was a Leyland Leopard with classic Alexander Y type coachwork, new to Midland Scottish.

The central belt of Scotland has long been fruitful territory for independent bus operation. Irvine (trading as Golden Eagle) of Salsburgh ran from their home village into Aidrie, using a fleet of AEC Reliance buses. After the demise of that marque, buses were sourced from other manufacturers, an example being F706WCS, a Volvo B10M with Duple 300 type bodywork. It's seen here in Airdrie town centre on a sunny day in spring 1991.

Allander of Milngavie was a long-established coach business to the north of Glasgow. Deregulation saw its expansion into stage carriage work, with operations under the name of Loch Lomond Coaches. The small town of Balloch, at the southern end of Loch Lomond, was served, but the main hub of the routes was the Clydeside town of Dumbarton. It is here, in summer 1993, that we see D375RHS, a Volvo B10M with Duple Dominant bus bodywork, new to another Scottish operator, Hutchison of Overtown.

The shores and lochs of the North Clyde estuary, east of Helensburgh, are today served by Wilson's of Rhu. Like many modern independents, they own a small fleet of Optare Solo buses like YJ57EGV, seen here sandwiched between Loch Long and the historic Knockderry House Hotel at Cove. On 22 September 2009, the bus is heading for Helensburgh and its journey will take it past Kilcreggan, Garelochhead, Faslane RN Dockyard and the depot at Rhu.

Hawkhead is a suburb of the Renfrewshire town of Paisley and was home to Graham's Bus Service. A 1976 visit to the depot found these two super Guy Arab buses. G5 (AXS431) is a 1958 Arab IV/Northern Counties, while the later G12 (FXS601) had rare Strachans bodywork. Sadly, Graham's, like all the 1970s Paisley independents, are no longer with us, though others have stepped in to take their place.

Paton Brothers, of Renfrew Ferry, ran services between the ferry terminal and Paisley town centre. At the depot, situated next to the famous Izzi's ice cream factory, is former Colchester 29 (MWC129), a Leyland PD2A/31 with Massey bodywork, photographed in 1978.

The last of the old order of Paisley independents was McGill's of Barrhead, which sold out to Arriva in 1997. Latterly a fleet of Leyland Nationals ran the bus services, but a much more unusual vehicle was this Leyland-DAB Artic. FHE291V was new to South Yorkshire Passenger Transport Executive and is seen here in central Glasgow in June 1986.

A1 Service was a co-operative formed by many small operators in Ayrshire. The main route was from Ardrossan to Kilmarnock, but there were also several local workings around the small town on the route served. It is on one of these that we see ex-Maidstone & District Volvo Ailsa/Alexander registered LKP381P, photographed in Stevenston in summer 1986. The Daimler Fleetline behind is owned by another co-operative, AA Buses (see below). A1 sold out to Stagecoach in 1995.

Since the 1970s, the AA Buses co-operative consisted of just two operators, Dodd's of Troon and Young's of Ayr. In the spring of 1981, Dodd's Dennis Dominator/East Lancs 'decker HCS31V was photographed in Stevenston, en route for Ayr, on the main route from Ardrossan. Stagecoach took over all AA routes in 1997, though Dodd's still exist as a thriving coach business.

The other member of AA Buses, Young's, ran services in and around Ayr. Here are a pair of Leyland Lynx single-deck buses, F85XCS and D573LSJ, at the terminal point in Ayr in spring 1991.

A third Ayrshire co-operative was Clyde Coast. In later years only single-deck vehicles were used, typically the Leyland Leopard with Plaxton Elite coachwork. NSD534L is about to depart from its terminus in Saltcoats for another seaside town, Largs, in June 1986. En route, it will pass its depot at West Kilbride.

Lanarkshire is an industrial area to the south-east of Glasgow, where many independent bus companies can still be found. Unfortunately, one of the larger ones, Hutchison's, sold their long-established stage services to First Group in 1997. A most unusual bus in this smart fleet was B948ASU, one of two Volvo B10M/Van Hool vehicles fitted with bus-type folding doors and bus seats. It is photographed here in the depot yard at Overtown, in June 1986. The bus was later operated by Beeston's of Hadleigh, Suffolk, and has recently been reported with Kenzie's of Shepreth, Cambridgeshire.

Wilson's of Carnwath, near Lanark, had a varied fleet of buses. An unusual Bedford minibus used on the 'Medwyn Gypsy' subsidised routes was XGE80S, seen here in the depot yard in spring 1981. A former Edinburgh Leyland PD3 used on contract services stands behind.

Mackies of Alloa run several routes around Clackmannanshire and into the city of Stirling. A modern fleet of low-floor buses is used for these duties. In September 1998, P739FMS, a Dennis Dart SLF/Caetano saloon, arrives in Stirling, with its blind set for the return journey.

The capital city of Scotland is not fertile ground for local independent bus operations, being dominated by Lothian Buses and the Scottish Bus Group, with Stagecoach and First taking on the latter's role today. The stage services of Edinburgh Transport did not last long, but I was able to photograph Leyland National SGR553R arriving into the bus station in spring 1991. The vehicle was new to Northern General.

Bus services in Dumfries use an area known as Whitesands as their terminus, alongside the River Nith. It is here that we see one of the local independents, Gibson's of Moffat. OJY573S was new to Trathen's of Yelverton, Devon. It is a Volvo B58 with a Plaxton Viewmaster coach body, not really suitable for the regular run to Moffat in early 1992. The company has recently given up its stage carriage work.

MacEwan's Coach Services run many services throughout southern Scotland, even reaching the capital. Here is one of their modern buses in its home town, Dumfries. SJ09GDV is a MAN with Wright Eclipse bodywork, caught on camera at Whitesands on 2 June 2011.

Perryman's Buses are based at Berwick-upon-Tweed, in England (though some would dispute that!), but run mainly northwards into Scotland, including a trunk service to Edinburgh. A modern fleet of low-floor buses is owned and a good example is seen here. Optare Solo CE52UXA passes the excellent Cross Inn at Paxton, just over the Scottish border, en route for Berwick on 26 September 2009.

On the same sunny day, Travelsure of Seahouses was running this Mercedes 814D/Plaxton minibus in Berwick-upon-Tweed. It was new to Surrey operator Tellings-Golden Miller, hence its registration P40TGM. Travelsure run many services along the Northumberland coast. This one is off to Holy Island (Lindisfarne), operating to a timetable dependant on the tide, as it will have to negotiate a causeway to reach its destination.

The market town of Hexham was once served by several independent bus companies. Some of them survive today, but not Rochester and Marshall of Great Whittington, as the business was bought by the Go Ahead Group. OCN897R, photographed in spring 1981 at Hexham bus station, is a typical rural coach of the time. It is a Bedford YLQ/Plaxton Supreme C45F with 'grant' doors for use on stage services.

The more industrial part of Northumberland is the coastal area to the south of Blyth. The mining village of Seaton Delaval was home to Hunter's Coaches, with a fascinating collection of mainly second-hand buses. To illustrate the fleet, I have chosen this photo of Metro-Scania double-decker OTN446R from Whitley Bay in late 1986. The bus was new to Tyne & Wear PTE, so did not travel far when bought by Hunter's.

One of my favourite North-Eastern operators was Economic, a consortium of two businesses, running the high frequency South Shields to Sunderland service. I am grateful to Jim Sambrooks for taking this excellent picture of Wilson's 2372PT, a 1961 AEC Reliance with Roe DR41F coachwork. It was photographed in Sunderland town centre in the early 1970s, on a short working to Hartburn.

Another Sunderland area bus company was W.H. Jolly, based at South Hylton. Bedfords were the favoured vehicle type, and this bus is no exception. BGR683W is a YMT with 53-seat Duple Dominant bus bodywork, bought new in 1980 and seen on a foggy day outside the depot in that year. The bus was later sold to Minsterley Motors of Shropshire. Both operators on this page were bought out by Tyne & Wear PTE.

Hylton Castle Coaches began services after deregulation, using the fleetname 'Catch A Bus' and running around Sunderland and South Shields. Leaving the latter, on a local route, is Dennis Dart/Plaxton K832SFT in summer 1993.

In the summer of 1988, Durham operator Bob Smith was using this ex-Wallace Arnold Leyland Leopard/Plaxton coach on the service to Langley Park, where the depot was situated. AUA419J was photographed in the city centre, with a backdrop of the railway viaduct.

Delta Coaches was a post-deregulation operator, running various services in the Stockton/ Middlesborough area. This former United Counties Bristol RELH6G/ECW, registered YNV205J, was found in Middlesborough town centre in June 1990, competing with Cleveland Transit.

The market town of Bishop Auckland was a fantastic place to find independent buses, as we will see in the next few pages. One of them was Lockey's, based at St Helens Auckland, in whose yard I photographed FCK884 in 1978. It was an ex-Ribble Motor Services Leyland Tiger Cub with Saunders Roe bus bodywork, which has since been preserved and restored to its original condition.

The largest independent in Bishop Auckland was OK Motor Services, with its main depot in the town centre. Services were operated locally and northwards to Newcastle. In the summer of 1980, the Market Place was host to PCW959, a Leyland Tiger Cub with East Lancs bodywork, new to Burnley, Colne and Nelson.

An unusual bus in the mainly Leyland OK fleet was TUP104V, a Northern Counties-bodied Dennis Dominator, seen in the summer of 1980 in the picturesque suburb of West Auckland. OK Motor Services sold out to the Go Ahead Group in 1995.

The number 6 has long been used by Weardale Motor Services as part of their bus registrations. Maintaining the tradition, this low-floor DAF/Ikarus carries W6WMS. It was photographed in Bishop Auckland's new bus station in the spring of 2002. Weardale, as the name suggests, run an hourly service along the Wear Valley to Stanhope, with some buses travelling beyond to the more rural villages.

Wright Brothers of Nenthead ran long-distance stage services between the North-East and the Lake District, plus some more local routes. Heading for the tiny Cumbrian town of Alston is Bedford YRQ/Plaxton Elite Express RRM915M, seen at Haltwhistle railway system in summer 1988.

Mountain Goat is an unusual company, specialising in tourist routes through the Lake District passes. Modern minibuses have long been in use, but here are two notable exceptions. Closest to the camera is HGA984D, a Bedford VAS1 with Willowbrook 24-seat bus body. It was new to the famous Scottish operator David MacBrayne, so would have been well used to mountainous terrain. Behind is a Bedford YRT/Duple coach LEC861P, formerly in the fleet of Stainton of Kendal. The location is Windermere railway station on a dull day in June 1983.

This long-established independent is, thankfully, still with us. Fishwick's of Leyland operate the Preston-Leyland-Chorley corridor. Given the location of their depot, it will come as no surprise that Fishwick's used a fleet of mainly Leyland buses. A classic example of these was fleet number 30 (ATB597A), a 1963 Leyland Atlantean PDR1/1 with Weymann body. It was photographed unloading opposite the railway station approach road in Preston in 1978. Fishwick's once built their own bodywork, under the Fowler name, and two of these buses are included later in this volume.

The East Lancashire town of Blackburn was once a stronghold of Ribble and the local municipals, but deregulation changed all that. Darwen Coach Services was just one of several independents that entered the fray. In Blackburn's bus station in September 2004, we find F917YWY, a Mercedes 811D with Optare StarRider coachwork, new to London Buses as SR16.

Pilkingtons was another post-deregulation operator in East Lancashire. In the spring of 1994, I found this Leyland National arriving in Accrington town centre. Though registered PIB6945, it was new to United Counties as GVV888N.

25

In 1979, when this photograph was taken, Lancashire United was the largest independent UK bus company. Sadly, that was not to last; the company was later absorbed into Greater Manchester Transport. On a typical autumn day, fleet number 100 (564TD), a 1962 Daimler Fleetline/Northern Counties, leaves the shelter of the former Lancashire & Yorkshire Railway bridge under Manchester Victoria Station.

The sun does shine in Manchester occasionally, even in autumn 2004. In the centre of the city, close to Piccadilly Gardens, we see Bluebird's MD02BLU, a Dennis Dart SLF, bodied by East Lancs. It's heading back to its home town of Middleton. Bluebird commenced stage services after deregulation and still operates today.

Mayne's of Droylsden ran a service into Manchester's Stevenston Square for many years. The company still exists, but recently sold its stage services to Stagecoach. A typical bus of the 1960s and '70s is this 1963 AEC Regent V/Neepsend 8859VR, seen opposite the depot during a crew change. It was photographed in June 1980, towards the end of its working life. Thankfully, this bus has been saved from the cutter's torch by a preservationist.

Stuart's was another post-deregulation bus company, running services from Manchester towards Ashton and Stalybridge. A sunny spring day in 1989 found JFR398N in Piccadilly Gardens, Manchester. It was a former Blackburn Transport Leyland Atlantean/East Lancs.

South Lancashire Transport is a resurrection of the name of a long-vanished trolleybus operator, but *this* SLT runs a sizeable fleet of buses in the area around Wigan and Leigh. T731DGD is a Dennis Dart/Marshall Capital bus, found in Leigh bus station. Behind is a little Dennis Dart MPD of another Leigh independent, Jim Stones.

ABC Travel was a small Merseyside bus company, with many tendered routes in Liverpool and beyond, even reaching into Yorkshire for a while. On a Formby local route is Optare Metrorider N8ABC, photographed at Freshfield Station in late 1996, just after a shower of rain. ABC was later absorbed into CMT (see below).

After 'D Day' in 1986, Liverpool became a hotbed of competition. One of many newcomers to the scene were CMT Buses, who owned this Leyland National, seen passing Lime Street Station in early 1992. UPB309S was new to London Country as its SNB309.

Another competitive independent was Liver Line, running a fleet of new and second-hand double deckers. From Strathclyde Buses came this Leyland AN68A/1R with Alexander bodywork, registered RUS304R, photographed in central Liverpool in summer 1988. Liver Line was taken over by North Western Road Car, now part of Arriva (owned by Deutsche Bahn).

Unlike the last two independents, Selwyn's of Runcorn ran only tendered services in the Liverpool area. Heading for Liverpool John Lennon (formerly Speke) Airport is X783NWX, a DAF/Wright Cadet saloon, seen in Liverpool city centre in June 2003. This particular vehicle later ended up with Arriva.

The Optare City Pacer, based on a Volkswagen LT55, was a product of the mid 1980s and purchased in large numbers by some companies. This particular one, D231TBW, was new to Oxfordshire operator South Midland. It later moved north to St Helens-based Town Flyers and is seen here in that town in spring 1994.

Another bus originally from the Oxford area was this dual-doored Bristol VR/ECW, PFC511W, new to City of Oxford Motor Services. In the hands of Wirral operator Happy Al's, it's seen entering Birkenhead's Woodside Ferry bus terminal in June 1995.

Now here is a really rare bird! It is a Ward Dalesman with Wadham Stringer bodywork, new as number 6 in the Darlington Transport fleet, seen here laying over in the parking area of Chester bus station. In spring 1995, when this photograph was taken, A106CVN was owned by Devaway, which ran services around Chester and the small inland towns of North Wales.

Wrexham has long been a town full of interesting independents. In the 1970s, several of these ran to the mining villages to the south of the Welsh town. Entering the stance area of Wrexham bus station is Phillip's DWA402H, a Ford R192/Willowbrook, which was new to Booth & Fisher of Halfway, Yorkshire, in 1970. It's photographed in August 1976.

To my knowledge, there have been at least three companies owned by various personages called Jones, which is strange considering there is no 'J' in the Welsh language! In the spring of 1995, E. Jones & Sons were the owners of this unusual Duple-bodied Leyland Cub, next to Lothian Regional Transport of Edinburgh, in whose fleet it was number 175. HSC175X is seen here in Wrexham bus station.

Another Wrexham independent, Wright's, expanded their network of services after deregulation. Prior to 1986, they ran a service to Penycae, where the small garage was situated. A Seddon single-decker was the regular performer in the mid 1970s. By 1982, a new livery had been introduced and this Volvo B58-56/Plaxton Bustler, GCA772X, had been bought new. I managed to capture it on the outskirts of Wrexham when it was almost new. With the expansion of the fleet, a new depot was established in an industrial estate on the edge of the town.

Bryn Melyn Motor Services was a small business with a depot in the picturesque Welsh town of Llangollen. The principal bus used on the stage services at the time (June 1978) was this fine Bedford SB5/Willowbrook 45-seater, CCA768L, seen here laying over in the town. Bryn Melyn gained new routes after deregulation and was later taken over by GHA Coaches, though some vehicles retain Bryn Melyn identities.

Llanhaeadr-yn-Mochnant is the village where most of the fleet of Tanat Valley is based. Services are operated around the Shropshire/Mid Wales borders area. One of the principal routes was the X75 Shrewsbury to Llanidloes and it is at its Welsh terminus that we see Optare Tempo integral YJ56ATX on 5 October 2010.

Earlier in this book we saw B948ASU, a Volvo B10M/Van Hool bus, with Hutchinson's of Overtown. Its sister, also new to Hutchison's, became A15RBL, after service in South Wales with Rhondda and Stagecoach. By May 2005, when I photographed it in Betws-y-Coed, A15RBL was in the hands of GHA Coaches, an operator that has greatly expanded into former Crosville territory over recent years.

Purple Motors of Bethesda and their subsidiary Deiniolen Motors served the valleys to the south of Bangor, a small city in North Wales. Regular performer on the Deiniolen route, FCK844, a Leyland Tiger Cub bodied by Saunders Roe, is seen here in Deiniolen in May 1978. The bus has since been preserved and restored to its original Ribble livery.

DED797 was new to Warrington Corporation in 1946 as number 18. It is a Leyland Titan PD1, with bodywork construction contracted out to Alexander's, to Leyland's design. By 1977, when I photographed it with Whiteways of Waenfawr, it was close to the end of its commercial life. Luckily, it has been preserved. Whiteways ran their main service into Caernarfon.

Caernarfon was a focal point for several independents. Clynnog & Trefor Motors operated the route southward to Pwllheli. A terribly wet Caernarfon day in mid 1979 is illustrated here as C&T's 255BKM prepares for departure from the main square. The bus is a 1958 AEC Reliance with Harrington coachwork, new to Maidstone & District.

Another Caernarfon-area independent now, with an ex-Maidstone & District AEC Reliance. 334NKT was bodied by Weymann, and after further use with Booth & Fisher and South Yorkshire PTE, it was purchased by Silver Star. It was used on their mountainous route up to Cesarea, where I photographed it among the slate piles in around 1982. A few years earlier, Silver Star had been using Bristol SC4LK saloons on this service.

We now take a quick trip over the Irish Sea to Northern Ireland, not an area known for independent buses. Nevertheless, a couple are illustrated here. Sureline of Lurgan was formed in 1965 to operate several routes to the surrounding towns and villages, which were about to be withdrawn by the Ulster Transport Authority. Seen in the spring sunshine of 1983 at the depot is CIB5372, a Ford with Sureline's own bodywork. Surely one of Ulster's most unusual buses? I am grateful to the *Lurgan Mail* for some helpful information.

The Londonderry & Lough Swilly Railway Company ceased running trains many years ago, but they still run bus services to this day, trading as Lough Swilly. Though Londonderry is the terminus of many of the routes, most of them cross the border into the Republic. On such duties is number 157, photographed in Derry bus station around 1982. Registered AUI7255, it was previously UCK511, which, as those who study such things will know, makes it a former Ribble vehicle (number 511). It is a 1964 Marshall-bodied Leyland Leopard, which was withdrawn and scrapped by Lough Swilly in 1983.

Back across the Irish Sea to south-west Wales, we arrive at Pembroke Dock, home of a large independent, Silcox. This company runs many routes throughout the area. For many years, Bristol buses were favoured, and in this picture of a depot yard taken in November 1975, several can be seen, along with a newish Leyland Leopard/Duple Dominant bus. Perhaps the most unusual vehicle though is PVO624, a rebodied ex-East Midland Leyland (second from left).

Another large independent in the area is Richards Brothers, based at Newport. One of their Carlyle-bodied Dennis Darts, H158HDE, passes through the village of Penparc, heading south in March 1995.

The poet and writer Dylan Thomas was a resident of Laugharne, near Carmarthen. The village was also the home of Pioneer Coaches. A visit to the depot yard in November 1975 found this pair of buses having a well-earned rest. FCH20 is a Leyland Tiger Cub/Weymann, new to Trent Motor Traction, while UTX9 is an ex-Caerphilly UDC Leyland Royal Tiger, bodied by Massey.

Here is a most unusual bus in the fleet of Jones of Login. D727GDE is an East Lancs-bodied Scania K92CRB, seen close to Carmarthen railway station, awaiting departure for Pendine in June 1989. It later saw further service with Rhodes of Yeadon, Yorkshire.

Eynon's, based at the village of Trimsaran, ran one of the inland routes between Llanelli and Carmarthen, serving their home village and the small town of Kidwelly. In a typical scene in the depot yard in 1978, here is a row of Leyland double-deck buses, plus a little Bedford coach. All the 'deckers are second-hand, starting life with (left to right) Bolton, Wallasey, Glasgow and Bradford. Eynon's later sold out to Davies of Pencader, who, in turn, were swallowed up by First Group.

Creamline's depot at Tonmawr occupied a perilous position overlooking a South Wales valley. A stage service was operated into the nearby town of Neath. Modern Leyland Leopards were used, but some older vehicles were retained for schools and contract duties. 2743AC was a Leyland Tiger Cub/ Willowbrook, new to Stratford Blue, seen here on the slope to the depot yard in June 1978. I hope the handbrake works!

Caerau is a former mining village at the head of a valley near Maesteg. A collection of corrugated iron sheds formed the depot of Brewer's Motor Services, though it was common for buses awaiting their next duty to be left on the road outside. AEC Reliances made up the majority of the fleet, though Leylands and Bedfords were also owned. KNY968L is a Reliance with Willowbrook 002 dual-purpose body, an unusual combination, photographed outside the depot in June 1978. Brewer's also maintained a small depot in Maesteg. When South Wales Transport/First Group took over, the Brewer's name was retained for several years and could be seen as far away as Cardiff and Swansea.

Llynfi Motor Services was a well-respected company running into Maesteg and Port Talbot. The depot was situated up a hill overlooking Maesteg and its colliery. The variety of buses in the fleet can be glimpsed in this photograph as 136 (AGA129B) arrives at the depot in June 1978. It is a Leyland Atlantean PDR1/1, with Alexander body, new as Glasgow Corporation LA190.

The main business of Bebb's of Llantwit Fadre was high-class coaching, but the company had long operated a local service into Pontypridd and an occasional foray into Cardiff. Deregulation brought an opportunity to expand bus services, including routes to the delights of Bridgend. However, it is in Pontypridd, on a rare sunny day in spring 1991, that we see G25HDW, loading up for Church Village. The bus is a Dennis Javelin with Duple 300 bus bodywork.

Thomas of Barry ran, for many years, a Cardiff to Barry stage service. The regular performer on this route was ATG708J, a Willowbrook-bodied Leyland Leopard. It is seen here, in 1977, in Cardiff bus station, waiting for departure time. The route was later taken over by Shamrock Buses, but they too have now vanished.

A company called John's Travel just *had* to feature in these pages! Local services are run in the Merthyr Tydfil area, mainly using minibuses. This Ford/Wadham Stringer saloon, DHV199Y, photographed at Merthyr bus station, autumn 1992, is an exception to that rule. I have tried researching the history of this bus, but to no avail. It is typical of many that were purchased by local authorities for welfare duties.

Glyn Williams of Cross Keys ran several stage carriage routes into Newport. Normally, a green colour scheme was employed, but T602DAX looks very smart in this silver livery to celebrate 25 years of the company. It is a 28-seat low-floor Dennis Dart with the usual Plaxton Pointer body, photographed passing through Rogerstone, en route for Newport, in the summer of 1999.

We travel back to England again and reach the cathedral city of Hereford. Also arriving here is this rural service operated by Sargeant's of Kington, a small market town near the Welsh border. Optare Solo Y877PWT is about to arrive at Hereford's Country Bus Station in the summer of 2004. At peak times, double deckers are used on this route.

The major independent operator in Hereford is locally based Yeoman's. In the summer of 1991, Dennis Dart/Carlyle 36-seater H554YCJ is seen on a local route in the city centre. Like many buses in this smart fleet, this one was bought new.

The small town of Bishops Castle was connected to the regional centre, Shrewsbury, by an hourly service operated by Valley Motor Services. Three typical members of the fleet are seen in the depot yard in Bishops Castle in 1980. From left to right these are KSD550F, a Ford R192 new to Paterson's of Dalry, KUX321P, a 1975 Ford R1114, and BAW958T, a Ford R1114/Duple coach. Valley MS no longer exists and the service is now operated by Minsterley Motors.

The flags are out in Bishops Castle in July 1999, not for the arrival of the Minsterley Motors bus from Shrewsbury, but for the town's annual festival. D918GRU was a Bedford YMT/Plaxton bus, new to Tillingbourne of Surrey.

272STF is a 1961 AEC Reliance/Plaxton dual-purpose saloon, new to Lancashire United. It is seen here in the ownership of Parish of Morda, Shropshire, at the depot in 1977. Parish ran a regular service into the nearby town of Oswestry.

This fine machine was the regular performer on a local service to Pulverbatch from Shrewsbury. KWX413 of Williamsons, an ancient Bedford SB/Duple Vega, is seen here at its Shrewsbury terminus in 1977, along with some Valley Motor Services saloons.

Boulton's of Cardington is an old Shropshire operator, which has sent buses into Shrewsbury for many years. Heading for that town, but arriving in Wellington bus station on a snowy March day in 2001, is this Mercedes 811D/Optare StarRider, E402YNT. It was bought new by Boulton's and later saw service with another Shropshire company, M&D Travel.

Martlews of Telford was one of a number of small companies who formed the Shropshire Omnibus Association, running various stage services around Wellington and the new town of Telford. In 1975, this fine old Bedford saloon, UUJ394, is seen at Donnington terminus, where it has just connected with the Happy Days service from Stafford. The entire operations of the Shropshire Omnibus Association were later taken over by Midland Red.

Leyland National AKU16oT was new to South Yorkshire Transport as number 1060, but is shown here in later life as number 75 with Birmingham Coach Company. In spring 1995, it was photographed in Birmingham city centre, passing the Square Peg, a Wetherspoon's pub, from where the Birmingham bus scene can be viewed.

Another operator running into England's second city was Burman Travel, which ran out towards Staffordshire. GBB985N, a former Tyne & Wear PTE Leyland Leopard/Alexander saloon, is seen here below New Street railway station in summer 1991.

Berresford's of Cheddleton had a marvellous variety of buses to operate their services into the towns of the Potteries. The depot yard was known for its collection of withdrawn buses as the company was seemingly reluctant to throw anything away. In Hanley bus station, in 1985, TDK543K was providing entertainment for enthusiasts. Ordered by Rochdale Corporation, it's an AEC Swift, bodied by Pennine; a rare combination indeed.

In contrast to Berresford's, Turner's of Brown Edge mostly bought their service buses new. Leyland Fleetline/Northern Counties AFA489S, typical of the fleet, is leaving its stance in Hanley bus station in summer 1980. The company was later taken over by Potteries Motor Traction, though the livery and fleet name lived on for a few years afterwards.

Newcastle-under-Lyme is a market town on the western edge of the Potteries conurbation and was served by a couple of pre-deregulation independents. The regular vehicle on Duggin's local service was TRE675L, a Seddon Pennine VI with Pennine 'Intercity' coach body, one of only two ever built. It is seen here in Ironmarket, Newcastle, in 1977.

Poole's Coachways was based at Alsagers Bank, high above Newcastle-under-Lyme and ran a regular service between the two places. One of several Leyland Leopards in the fleet was XFA967S, the last bus purchased before the company's demise. It carried unusual Marshall bodywork, to the 'Camair' style. Here it is in Newcastle bus station during a cold snap in March 1979.

Just outside the Staffordshire town of Uttoxeter is a place called Spath, well known by bus enthusiasts as being the headquarters of Stevenson's. I first came across the company when its main operation was the Burton-on-Trent to Uttoxeter route. Expansion came in the 1980s, particularly when East Stafford District Council (formerly Burton Corporation) sold their fleet, services and depot to Stevenson's. It's on one of the Burton local services that we see fleet number 81 (F181YDA), an MCW Mark 2 Metrobus, originally a demonstrator, photographed in the town centre in summer 1989. British Bus later took over Stevenson's, retaining the name and expanding the network, which reached Manchester and Wolverhampton. The operations are now part of Arriva.

Harper Brothers of Heath Hayes, Staffordshire, ran several services around Cannock, plus two routes to Birmingham. It is at the terminus of both routes in 'Brum', Carrs Lane, that we see 23 (NRF349F), a 1968 Leyland Titan PD3/5 with Northern Counties H40/32RD body. It will shortly depart on the 944 route to Boney Hay, an operation that was shared with WMPTE (Walsall). Harper Brothers succumbed to the might of Midland Red in 1974. Thanks to Jim Sambrooks for taking the photograph and to Paul Roberts for most of the above information.

Warstone's Green Bus Service was another Staffordshire bus company, operating out of its base at Great Wyrley. Leaving the depot yard in 1982 is 521CTF, a rare Leyland Olympian saloon, new to Fishwick's of Leyland. It has since passed into preservation and been restored to Fishwick's colours. The Green Bus Service ran various routes, mainly into Wolverhampton.

Back in the 1970s, there were three independent companies regularly serving the city of Leicester. Gibson Brothers and Astill & Jordan had succumbed by the 1980s, but Hylton & Dawson of Glenfield managed to keep going into the twenty-first century. They have since given up their stage carriage work. In early 2002 I photographed this Plaxton Derwent saloon, re-registered as HDZ101, passing St Margaret's bus station in central Leicester.

The re-registration of buses is a pain in the proverbial for bus enthusiasts as it causes problems in researching the history and full details of such vehicles. I have, therefore, been unable to provide the full history of this Leyland National of Paul S. Winson, a Leicestershire operator running services in the Loughborough area. PIJ8104 was photographed in Loughborough itself in the spring of 1992.

2011 saw a famous Derbyshire independent giving up stage carriage work. Felix of Stanley had run the Derby to Ilkeston route for many years, latterly jointly with the Wellglade Group, now in sole charge of the service. Bedford VAM70/Plaxton Derwent bus GNU699H was found in Derby bus station in 1977, loading up for Ilkeston. Derby bus station was a classic 1930s structure, but has since been demolished and replaced by a modern facility.

Barton was once one of Britain's largest independent bus companies, with a headquarters at Chilwell, just outside Nottingham. The company also had several other depots and outstations. Until the mid 1970s, Barton ran a fascinating fleet of buses, though standardisation had begun, aided by the government's Bus Grant Scheme. One vehicle, typical of the time, bought with grant aid was this Leyland Leopard/Plaxton Supreme Express coach, number 542, seen here at Nottingham's Broadmarsh bus station in spring 1980. Barton was taken over by Trent Motor Traction, now part of the Wellglade Group.

A former Bristol Omnibus Company Bristol VR with dual-door ECW bodywork has found a second life in Nottingham city centre in early 1994. Number 1525 (PHY695S) was photographed while operating for Nottingham Omnibus, a short-lived subsidiary of Sheffield Omnibus, later to be taken over by Yorkshire Traction.

G.K. Kinch of Mountsorrel commenced most of its services after deregulation, running south to Leicester and north to Nottingham. Arriving at Nottingham in spring 1993 is HIL7773, a Leyland Leopard, with a much newer Willowbrook Warrior body. Kinchbus is now part of the Wellglade Group.

W. Gash & Son of Newark ran two services between Newark and Nottingham, one direct and the other via the villages. Until 1979, when an Atlantean arrived, the double-deck fleet consisted of front-engined Daimlers, which maintained the front-line duties. The oldest of these was DD1 (KAL578), a Massey-bodied CVD6, seen here in Newark bus station on the direct service to Nottingham, 1978. Gash sold out to Lincolnshire Road Car in 1989. Newark bus station has since been rebuilt. Thankfully, some of the Gash Daimlers were saved for preservation.

Another local operator has adopted the former Gash numbering system. Marshall's of Sutton-on-Trent own DD63 (P353ROO), a Volvo Olympian with East Lancs bodywork, new to Harris of Grays, Essex. It's seen here on a local route crossing the town bridge over the Trent in Newark on 3 April 2009. Marshall's now operate a regular Newark-Nottingham service.

Hulley's of Baslow have long operated the Chesterfield to Bakewell route; on these duties is FKF924F, photographed in Chesterfield in the summer of 1979. The bus was new to Liverpool Corporation as number 1045 and is an MCW-bodied Leyland Panther, never the most reliable of Leyland's products. Surprisingly, Chesterfield Transport also bought some similar vehicles. Today Hulley's operate several other routes, including regular visits to Sheffield.

Andrew's of Sheffield was originally a PSV training organisation, with a small fleet of AEC Regent V's. Stage operations commenced just after deregulation, using an ex-Douglas Corporation Mark V, the last one built I believe. Expansion followed and buses with rear engines were purchased, with each bus carrying a name, rather than a fleet number. 'Charlie Peace' (GWA810N) is seen passing a Sheffield Omnibus Leyland Atlantean outside Pond Street bus station in spring 1993. It is a Daimler Fleetline, new to South Yorkshire PTE as number 810. It carries an almost unique style of Eastern Coach Works bodywork, built only for the PTE and Colchester Transport. The company was later taken over by Yorkshire Traction.

Another Sheffield area operator was Booth & Fisher, with a modern depot at Halfway, near Beighton. Two main routes were operated, one to Sheffield, the other to Worksop, the latter often operated by Albion Nimbuses. At the depot in 1977 was WRA12, a rare AEC Monocoach, which has since entered preservation. Soon afterwards, Booth & Fisher sold out to South Yorkshire PTE.

Northern Bus Company metamorphosed from a previous Sheffield-area operator, Wigmore's of Dinnington. NBC were well known for running a fleet of Bristol RE buses and coaches, but a more unusual vehicle was this Leyland Leopard with Willowbrook coach 49-seat bodywork. WWY70X, seen here at Meadowhall Interchange in July 1994, was new to West Riding.

Dearneways of Goldthorpe introduced a service from the Dearne Valley towns directly into Sheffield. Prior to the company being taken over by SYPTE, a fleet of modern Leyland Leopard/ Plaxton coaches was employed on these duties. AWJ293T was a 51 seater, seen here in Sheffield bus station on a cold day in early 1981.

Despite having two large covered bus stations, services eastwards from Doncaster terminated in the open at Christchurch. Passenger and crew needs were satisfied by public toilets and Coopland's café – a breakfast here was basic, but *very* filling! No doubt the crew of Felix Motors' number 43 (932BWR) were enjoying some sustenance as I photographed their bus in 1977. 43 was one of a number of similar AEC Regent V's with Roe bodywork, based at the Hatfield depot. Altogether, since the 1960s, six independents used Christchurch as a terminus. Sadly there is insufficient space to illustrate them all and only one survives today, Selwyn Motors, while the others were taken over by South Yorkshire PTE.

Severn's of Dunscroft, once known as 'Cressy', ran eastwards out of Doncaster towards Thorne and Moorends. A fleet of Leyland double-deck buses was used on the main routes. The first Atlantean in the fleet was XWU890G, a PDR1/1 with Roe H44/31F bodywork. For some reason it carried an Albion-style badge, rather than the standard Leyland scroll. It's seen here at Christchurch terminus in 1976. First Bus now uses the former Severn's depot.

59

Leaving the South Bus Station in Doncaster is this Daimler Fleetline/Roe of Leon Motors, based at Finningley. It was photographed on a sunny day in 1986. 'Donny' to Finningley was Leon's main route, while other services ran to Misson and Wroot. Fleet number 105 (SWT433L) was new to Felix of Hatfield and was included in the sale to SYPTE. Leon eventually sold out to Mass, a Sheffield and Lincolnshire operator, though First now operate most of the services.

Doncaster's other bus station, the northern one, is host to South Yorkshire Road Transport's number 95 (DWX395T), a Leyland Fleetline/Northern Counties. Its route to Leeds will take it through Pontefract and Castleford, a journey of about 90 minutes' duration. The company's depot was in Pontefract, actually in *West* Yorkshire. After 95 was sold, it ended up with another Pontefract operator, Stringer's Coaches. SYRT was taken over by West Riding/Caldaire Group and the services are now in the hands of Arriva.

A consortium of three companies ran the Doncaster to Wakefield route, trading as United Services. By 1980, only one of the three survived, W.R. & P. Bingley, who owned this Plaxton Derwent-bodied saloon, DWW433H, seen in Wakefield bus station in that year. Despite the AEC badge on the front, it was in fact a Leyland Leopard, bought new. West Yorkshire PTE took over the company in the mid 1980s.

Another Leyland Leopard/Plaxton bus, a 55-seat 'Derwent', is seen here outside its depot in December 1978. The last traditional Barnsley-area independent, Larratt Pepper of Thurnscoe, owned AWW675G and it was a regular performer on the Barnsley run.

Here is a most unusual bus for an independent. It's a Wadham Stringer-bodied Dennis Lancet, SDW237Y, new to Merthyr Tydfil Transport in 1983. I found it on Bradford Interchange in autumn 1990. It was owned by a Barnsley-area independent, Pride of the Road. The company ran several services in the Barnsley, Wakefield and Leeds areas, but has since ceased trading.

Recent years have seen the re-appearance of the name 'Halifax Joint Committee'. Neither the corporation nor British Railways had any involvement in the new company as it is a true independent, though the green and orange livery is close to the original. AEC Routemasters and MCW Metrobuses were used in the past, but more recently former Dublin Olympians and second-hand Dennis Darts maintained the services. An example of the latter, photographed in Halifax by Jim Sambrooks in summer 2009, is K995CBO, a Wright Handybus, purchased from Stagecoach Red & White.

Another Yorkshire post-deregulation operator was Ivy Coaches, running around the Huddersfield and Halifax area, plus the nearby small towns. An extraordinary purchase was VDW445K, a 1972 Metro-Scania saloon, new to Newport Transport. It's seen here in the old bus station in Halifax in summer 1987.

At the time of writing (late 2011), I've learnt that Longstaff's of Mirfield have ceased running their long-established Mirfield to Dewsbury service. Seen here in Mirfield in autumn 1983 is VCX340X, a Leyland Atlantean AN68C/2R with Northern Counties H4736F body, bought new a year earlier.

Black Prince was a well-respected independent that took advantage of deregulation and commenced operations on the Leeds-Morley corridor. The company was, perhaps, best known for its fleet of Volvo Ailsa 'deckers. Here's a good example, seen passing the Corn Exchange in Leeds early in 1994. Number 94 (KSD94W) was new to Western SMT and carried the normal style of Alexander bodywork.

Pennine Motors of Gargrave ran a service through their home village, running between Skipton and Lancaster. Heading for Lancaster is this 1972 Plaxton Elite Express C49F-bodied Leyland Leopard, one of several in the fleet. OWR265K was photographed in Gargrave in the spring of 1981. Pennine Motors still operate today, though Lancaster is no longer served. On the plus side, a regular service now runs to Burnley.

The vehicles of York Pullman were a familiar sight in York until the 1980s. Services ran eastwards towards Stamford Bridge and north in the direction of Easingwold. The depot was within the city walls, in a quiet back street off Walmgate. Inside, in the spring of 1984, I found number 107 (FDN583S), a Roe-bodied Leyland Fleetline in an unusual reversed livery. I'm pleased to report that a new York Pullman has now appeared, and the traditional colours can be seen once again on tourist open top buses and modern stage carriage vehicles.

A newer operator in York is Stephenson's of Easingwold, with a modern fleet of smart buses. On 10 April 2010, this Scania L113CRL with East Lancs B49F body, P653VWX, was found laying over in York. It was new to another Yorkshire operator, Black Prince of Morley.

Back in the 1970s, Jaronda Travel ran a Selby to Drax service, but then took over the operations and depot of Majestic (Burley's), therefore gaining an hourly Selby-Cawood-York route. Just arrived in Selby on a clear winter's day in 1989 is DTL544T, a former Lincolnshire Road Car Bristol LH6L/EWC B43F. It is standing outside the excellent little café that serves the town's bus passengers, while Selby Abbey is prominent in the background. Jaronda later sold out to Arriva, the principal operator in Selby.

Appleby's Coaches was a north Lincolnshire operator with some stage routes into Grimsby. Deregulation brought expansion over the Humber, with services operating around Hull, Bridlington and here, in Scarborough. The coastline here features two bays, separated by a headland, so the seafront bus service has long been popular. On these duties in the summer of 1992 is 869NHT, an open-top Bristol FS6G. It was new to the Bristol Omnibus Company in 1961 and was originally fitted with a removable roof for seafront duties at Weston-super-Mare. My thanks to Jim Sambrooks for taking this photograph.

The small town of Goole is an unusual place. It is an inland port, built to serve the Aire & Calder Canal with coal being transferred between 'Tom Pudding' canal tubs and sea-going vessels. To the east and south are the flatlands drained by the Dutchman, Vermuyden, now a fertile agricultural area stretching into Lincolnshire. Goole has long been the boundary point between the various bus operators, large and small, and remains so even today. Not far away is the village of Newport, once served by the Hull & Barnsley Railway and later home to Holt's Coaches. This company ran an infrequent service into Goole, where, sometime around 1981, GXS621 was captured on film. It was a Daimler Fleetline, bodied by Alexander, and new to Grahams of Hawkhead, Paisley.

Good News Travel, trading as Metro, was a company that ran competitive services in the city of Kingston-upon-Hull. About to enter Ferensway bus station in spring 1990 is Leyland National NPD149L. It was new to London Country as LNC49 and had passed through the hands of Solihull District prior to arriving on Humberside.

The North Lincolnshire steel-making town of Scunthorpe is home to a few independent bus companies. Two of these once served the suburban route to Ashby. On such duties in 1979 at 'Scunny's' old bus station is Ubique's DFU95L. It's a 1972 Bedford YRQ/Willowbrook DP45F, bought new. Ubique no longer trades, but the other operator, Hornsby's (see below) is still in business and serving Ashby today.

Two DAF/Wright saloons of Hornsby's are seen here in Scunthorpe's rebuilt bus station in November 2009. YG52CGZ was bought new, but Y466HUA was new to a Cambridgeshire independent, Myall's of Bassingbourne. As well as Ashby (where the depot is sited), Hornsby's serve other destinations in North Lincolnshire.

Here is a vehicle that has had a lot of owners! TWJ342Y was new in 1983 to Chesterfield Transport, but then passed through the hands of two other council operators, Ipswich and Warrington. It has also operated for Express Motors of North Wales. It's seen here in the ownership of Hunt's of Alford, Lincolnshire, in Skegness in May 1996. The bus is a Dennis Falcon with East Lancs coachwork.

The small towns of the south-east-Lincolnshire flatlands are served by Fowler's of Holbeach Drove. Here, in Holbeach, in the summer of 1987, is VNB225L, formerly number 7254 in the Greater Manchester Transport fleet. It is a 1973 Daimler Fleetline with Northern Counties H43/32F body.

Reliance of Great Gonerby once operated a good number of local services in and around Grantham. On such duties, in the old bus station, is PTL625H, an AEC Reliance with Plaxton Derwent bodywork, photographed in early 1978. A new bus station has since been constructed on a different site, while Reliance no longer trades.

In the 1950s, Kime's of Folkingham were well known by RAF personnel as providers of leave transport at Lincolnshire's many airfields. Since then, stage carriage operations have expanded, taking the green buses to Boston, Grantham, Peterborough and the county of Rutland. The Kime family sold the business to the employees, but Centrebus have now taken over. Prior to that, in October 2010, YAZ8774 was photographed in Spalding's spacious bus station waiting to depart for Boston. This Volvo Olympian/Alexander was new to Dublin Bus as RH53 (registered 90-D-1053) at Clontarf Garage.

Wing's of Sleaford ran a local route serving the Lincolnshire town. Seen here in June 1986, passing the Carre Arms near Sleaford Station is GVO548K, a Bristol RELL6g/ECW B44D. It was new to East Midland Motor Services as number O548.

Perhaps the best-known Lincolnshire independent is Delaine of Bourne. The vehicles here are always immaculate and fleet number 141 (AD56DBL) is no exception. It is a Volvo B9TL low-floor bus, with East Lancs bodywork to the 'Olympus' style, seen in Bourne town centre loading up on the trunk route to Peterborough on 30 May 2009. Other services are also operated, taking blue buses to Stamford and elsewhere.

Morley's ran a regular Peterborough to Whittlesey route, with extensions to Coates and Turves. In Whittlesey's Market Place is CUL92V, a Leyland Titan, once T92 in the London Transport fleet. Morley's no longer trade, but a Peterborough-Whittlesey service is still operated by Embling's of Guyhirn.

Embling's operate several routes around the fenland towns of Wisbech and March. In the main square of the latter town we see A61XFW, a former Ministry of Defence Leyland Tiger/Marshall Campaigner, having just arrived from Wisbech in early 2002.

Kings Lynn is the largest town in north-west Norfolk and attracts independents from both Norfolk and South Lincolnshire, especially on market days. Dack's (Rosemary Coaches) were regular visitors to Lynn. Their main depot was at Terrington, but the former yard of Doughty's in Kings Lynn was also used. To illustrate the fleet, here is JPA183K, an AEC Reliance with Park Royal dual-purpose bodywork. It was new to London Country as RP83, one of a batch bought for Green Line service in the Home Counties. It is seen in Kings Lynn bus station in 1982.

Today Norfolk Green is the largest operator in the Kings Lynn area, having ousted First Group from the town. The company has greatly improved its bus services, particularly along the north Norfolk coast. On these duties is this Optare Solo 32-seater YK08EUC, seen in Brancaster Staithe, heading for Hunstanton on 15 May 2010.

The Norfolk village of Caston was once home to the vehicles of Colin S. Pegg, who ran a service into Kings Lynn. Representative of the smart fleet was 858GNM, a Willowbrook-bodied AEC Reliance, seen at the depot in the spring of 1978. The bus was new, in 1962, to H&C of Garston, near Watford.

Culling's Coach Services ran a couple of rural routes from Norwich. This Bedford YRQ/ Willowbrook B52F, UCL826K, was bought new for this purpose in 1972 and is seen here having a rest in the depot yard in Norwich city centre in 1977.

Over the last few years, Sander's Coaches have increased their presence in the Norwich and North Norfolk area with a fleet of modern buses. PLo8YMA is a Volvo B9TL with Optare Olympus bodywork, photographed in central Norwich on 2 April 2009. It did not last long with Sanders and soon passed to Ensignbus in Essex.

Great Yarmouth, on the Norfolk coast, was once home to a post-deregulation independent with an imaginative fleet name – Flying Banana. It was a minibus operation, competing with Great Yarmouth Transport and First Eastern Counties in the late 1980s and early 1990s. On a fine summer's day in 1990, E237VOM was photographed in the town centre. This Freight Rover Sherpa carried a Carlyle 20-seat body.

9DER was the first rear-engined bus to operate in the Cambridge area. It was owned by Burwell & District and was a Willowbrook-bodied Daimler Fleetline. It was photographed in Cambridge's Drummer Street bus station in 1977, about to depart for Burwell, where the depot was situated. After withdrawal it was bought for preservation and attended several rallies. Sadly, it was then broken up, but the cab area now forms an exhibit in Burwell Museum.

Premier Travel was the largest independent operator in the Cambridge area. The company was well known for its long distance coach services, but also ran a number of local stage carriage routes, towards Haverhill and Royston. Sometime around 1970, Jim Sambrooks took this photograph of VDV806, fleet number 202, at Drummer Street bus station. It was new to Devon General as SR806, a 1957 AEC Reliance/Weymann B41F, one of several in the Premier Travel fleet.

This is perhaps the most unusual bus in this entire book! B931KWM is a Quest 80, new to Merseyside PTE in 1985, number 0086. It would be fair to say that the Quest was not the most reliable of buses and MPTE soon sold their batch. The one seen here, labelled as the 'Noddy Bus', is seen here in Cambridge city centre in 1989, on a competitive service operated by Miller Brothers of Foxton. Millers' routes were soon taken over by Stagecoach Cambus, but the company still trades, now operating as Andrew's Coaches. Amazingly, a similar Quest bus was retained for preservation and still resides in the depot yard today.

One Cambridge area independent that still survives is Go Whippet, running between Cambridge, St Ives and Huntingdon, serving the many villages en route. A small share of the services along the new guided busway is also undertaken, using new single-deck buses. On the traditional route, leaving the rebuilt bus station in Cambridge, is FE51RAU. Photographed on 24 April 2009, it is an East Lancs-bodied Volvo B7TL, bought new.

The small Suffolk town of Long Melford lost its rail services many years ago, but the old station yard played host to the buses of Theobald's Coaches. In 1977, JKE336E was found here, bearing silver paint to help the Queen celebrate her Jubilee. The bus is a Massey-bodied Leyland Atlantean PDR1/1, new to Maidstone Corporation. Theobald's ran several routes in the local area, but no longer trades.

Norfolk's of Nayland ran an hourly service into Colchester, until being taken over by Hedingham Omnibuses. The fleet consisted mainly of second-hand vehicles, such as this ex-City of Oxford 1960 AEC Reliance/Park Royal B44F. 759KFC is seen here, parked in Nayland village in 1980.

Galloway of Mendlesham has long operated rural services as well as a fleet of coaches. In recent years stage carriage work has increased and the smart buses can be regularly seen in Ipswich and Bury St Edmunds. Between the two towns is Stowmarket, where I found AY55DGV parked outside the town's historic railway station on the last day of March 2011. Bought new by Galloway, it is a DAF/VDL SB120 with 39-seat Wright bodywork.

If one wants to photograph independent buses, then Sudbury, Suffolk, is undoubtedly one of the best places to go. Several companies serve the small bus station, including Chambers' of Bures, who operate the long Colchester-Sudbury-Bury St Edmunds route. Heading for Bury is JRT710N, a Bedford YRT/Plaxton bus, seen here in September 1983. Behind the bus is St Peter's church, one of three churches in the small town because Sudbury is split up into three parishes.

We've already seen this bus within these pages. B948ASU was new to Hutchison of Overtown, Scotland, but is now seen in the hands of Beeston's of Hadleigh, Suffolk. The rare Volvo B10M/ Van Hool bus was photographed entering the Cattle Market bus station in Ipswich in early 1999. Beeston's operate several services in the local area.

Hedingham Omnibuses is today a major independent in the Colchester area, having taken over several other operators, including Norfolk's of Nayland and Osborne's of Tollesbury. Fleet number L248 (HJB455W) was found in Colchester bus station in early 2004. New to Alder Valley as 635, it is a Bristol VRT with standard ECW bodywork. After service with Hedingham, the bus passed to BBC Wales and achieved fame in a Doctor Who production. It has since been preserved. Colchester bus station has changed over the years, being much reduced today. It was once covered by a multi-storey car park, but that had gone by the early twenty-first century.

The large village of Tollesbury was home to Osborne's, who ran regular routes to Colchester, Witham and Maldon. Arriving in Maldon in the spring of 1990 was GSL901N, a former Dundee Daimler Fleetline/Alexander 'decker. Osborne's were taken over in 1997 and the modern depot premises in Tollesbury are still in use by Hedingham Omnibuses.

Grays is an industrial Essex town on the north bank of the River Thames and is now served by a couple of independents. One of these is Imperial of Rainham, the proud owners of OJD837Y, a former London Buses MCW Metrobus, once numbered M837. It is seen here passing Grays railway station in the summer of 2004, heading for Lakeside Shopping Centre.

As well as being a dealer, Ensignbus operated several tendered routes in the Greater London area during the late 1980s and into the '90s. In the summer of 1990, FUT38V was found in Romford. This MCW Metrobus was new to Leicester City Transport. These services were later transferred to Capital Citybus, then on to First Group. However, Ensignbus now operate stage carriage services around Grays.

SM Travel has recently expanded operations in the Harlow area, with a regular route reaching Hertford. Leaving the bus station in that town on 21 February 2009 is P677RWU, a Dennis Dart SLF with Plaxton Pointer 35-seat body. It was new to Armchair of Brentford, West London.

Shortly after deregulation, Sampson's of Cheshunt commenced suburban operations in Welwyn Garden City, Hertfordshire. Seen at the old bus station there in summer 1987 is TOR464N. This Daimler Fleetline/East Lancs was new to West Midlands PTE as number 4463. It will soon depart on HCC tendered route G3.

On the same day, E511PWR, a Volkswagen LT55/Optare City Pacer 25-seater of Welwyn Hatfield Line is photographed leaving Welwyn Garden City bus station on a local route. WHL ran several routes in the town at the time, but were soon taken over by London Country North East. The bus station in Welwyn Garden City has since been relocated, in conjunction with the construction of a new shopping centre and railway station entrance.

A Bedfordshire operator, Buffalo of Flitwick, once ran several routes in neighbouring Hertfordshire. Heading for St Albans is A698EAU, a Leyland Olympian with Northern Counties bodywork to a design specified by its original owner, Nottingham City Transport, where it was numbered 698. It has just passed under the former Midland Railway's Hemel Hempstead branch in Redbourn in the summer of 1991.

Deep in London Country territory, Rover Bus Service ran a Hemel Hempstead to Chesham (where the company was based) service for many years. On a bright spring day in 1987, 622JJO was photographed in Hemel bus station. New as VUR118W to Ward's of Epping, Essex, it was a 1980 Ford R1114 with B53F Duple Dominant body. Thanks to Michael Penn for assistance with this information.

Perhaps the most loved Buckinghamshire bus operator was Red Rover. The company was, unfortunately, taken over by Luton & District, now part of Arriva. At the main depot yard in Aylesbury, in the spring of 1978, three AEC buses are parked up. The two double deckers, DAU383C and DAU358C, are ex-Nottingham Renowns with MCW bodies, while in the middle is 8626DT, a former Doncaster AEC Reliance/Roe. The latter was one of a small batch of such vehicles that did not find favour in Doncaster and was sold off early. Red Rover ran several services radiating out of Aylesbury.

A recent addition to the scene in Buckinghamshire is Carousel Buses. The company runs several routes around High Wycombe, reaching Uxbridge and even Heathrow Airport. Closer to home, RX60DLZ was photographed leaving Chesham town centre on 30 October 2010. This Alexander Dennis Enviro bus is based on a MAN 14.240 chassis and is numbered ENV17 in the smart Carousel fleet.

Two former London buses re-united! At Gloucester Green bus station in Oxford in spring 1983, MLH402L of Charlton Services meets Mott's OJD226R. MLH is a Daimler Fleetline, DMS1402 with London Transport, while OJD is a later Leyland Fleetline, previously DMS2226. Charlton Services ran into Oxford from a base in the Oxfordshire village of Charlton-on-Otmoor and still trade today, while Buckinghamshire operator Mott's no longer run stage services. Gloucester Green bus station has now been redeveloped and serves as Oxford's busy coach station.

The Royal Borough of Windsor was once home to an independent. Imperial ran lightweight buses on a couple of local routes. Typical of the fleet at the time, around 1981, was LMR735F, a Bedford VAM70 bodied by Willowbrook. It was new to Wilts & Dorset as number 815, part of a small batch of such vehicles, providing some variety in the Bristol-dominated fleet.

Guildford, in Surrey, was home to several independents, including Tillingbourne, a company running several routes to the south and east of the town. Loading up for Peaslake at its Guildford terminal point in 1976 is the Leyland Leopard/Roe B49F, LWU499D. The bus was new to another famous independent, Pennine of Gargrave, Yorkshire.

BET Company Southdown ran green buses throughout Sussex, but that company vanished after the sale of the National Bus Company. A new Southdown has now emerged, an independent named 'Southdown PSV'. Several services are operated, mainly around Crawley, but also into Surrey. The town of Redhill is in that county and it was here, on a sunny 27 January 2009, that I photographed GX06AOE, an East Lancs-bodied Volvo B7TL, bought new in 2006.

The Kentish town of Sevenoaks was once the meeting point of London Country and Maidstone and District buses. The sale of the National Bus Company and deregulation changed all that. One of the 'new wave' of independents was Auto-Reps. Their bus, JPA149K, is seen here in the spring of 1990 in Sevenoaks bus station, ready to leave for Borough Green, former M&D territory. Ironically, the bus is an ex-London Country AEC Reliance with Park Royal dual-purpose bodywork, once RP49 in that fleet.

The town of Faversham in Kent is known for its brewing activities and it is appropriate that the closed Whitbread Brewery forms the backdrop to this photograph. In the foreground, in early 1993, is KJD542P of Westbus. It is a former London Transport (LS42) dual-doored Leyland National.

Another former London bus operating in Faversham. Donsway's AEC Swift (or Merlin as LT called them) AML570H is seen passing the town's railway station in early 1982. Formerly MB570 in the LT fleet, it carries MCW bodywork.

Rambler of Hastings ran a few stage carriage services in its home town and operating one of these, heading for Rye, is CKN143Y, photographed in the Hastings town centre in 1993. It's a former Maidstone Boro' line Bedford YMT/Wright DP53F; quite a rare vehicle.

The ex-London AEC Swift was not popular with operators, but Hants & Sussex loved them! Arriving at Havant bus station in February 1993 is AML97H, new to London Transport as SMS99. Hants & Sussex is no longer in business.

Another independent to serve the Hampshire town of Havant is Emsworth and District. In the summer of 2000, Leyland Swift/Reebur B39F H37YCW arrives in town. It was new in 1990 as number 37 in the Hyndburn Transport fleet, Accrington, Lancashire.

No book on British independents would be complete without a mention of New Canal, a street used as a termination/boarding point by various independents operating into Salisbury. At this location is former Accrington Corporation Bristol RESL6L/East Lancs STC928G, one of four bought by Brutonian, of Bruton, Somerset. The bus was captured on film in the spring of 1984, still in its municipal colours.

Cottrell's of Mitcheldean, Gloucestershire, ran a regular service into the county town until the early twenty-first century. Reversing out of Gloucester bus station in the autumn of 1991 is this MCW Metrobus, GBU6V, heading for Cinderford in the Forest of Dean. The bus was new to Greater Manchester Transport in 1979 as fleet number 5006.

Another Gloucestershire independent was Swanbrook, based at Staverton, between Cheltenham and Gloucester. Optare Solos tend to be used on stage services today, but back in May 1980, two more interesting buses were photographed in the depot. TTJ496M and WTE485L were both unusual single-deck Daimler Fleetlines from Fishwick's of Leyland, Lancashire. Each bus has Fishwick's own Fowler bodywork.

Bere Regis & District was a fascinating company for bus enthusiasts. In the firm's latter years, a model bus, cosmetically restored, greeted visitors to the headquarters in Dorchester. The yard to the rear always contained a wonderful selection of Bedford SB types, which were used on the many rural stage services. Three such coaches were found here in 1977. YWW549 carries Harrington coachwork, UFR123 has a Burlingham body, while a Duple example is on WMB461. The Bere Regis name finally vanished into history in 1995, though most of the company was sold a year earlier.

Two young ladies of South Petherton are captured on film in 1975, along with WYD306H, an AEC Reliance with 45-seat Willowbrook bodywork. This bus belongs to Hutchings & Cornelius, based in the Somerset village. The company's main route was from Yeovil to Taunton, via South Petherton. The company ceased trading in the late 1970s.

At Yeovil bus station, one could travel onwards to Shepton Mallet using Wake's Coaches, based at Sparkford, Somerset. The company favoured lightweight buses, such as this Bedford YRQ/Willowbrook, VUJ252J, seen arriving at Yeovil in early 1984. The bus was new to Brown of Donnington Wood, where it had been used on Shropshire Omnibus Association services. Like most of the twentieth-century Yeovil independents, Wake's no longer operate.

Filer's of Ilfracombe, Devon, ran competitive services around their home town, to Barnstaple and Bideford. A most unusual bus found in Barnstaple in the summer of 1997 was J227OKX, an Iveco Turbocity with bodywork by Alexander. It was new in 1991 as an Iveco Demonstrator.

Devon operator Tally Ho! is one of only a few British bus companies to have an exclamation mark in the fleet name. Though based in Kingsbridge, a large depot was maintained at Ivybridge, where SPK117M was found in 1982. This ECW-bodied Bristol LH was new to London Country as BL17 and would have performed similar duties for both companies.

In the 1990s and the first few years of the twenty-first century, Truronian expanded stage carriage operations in the Truro area. Loading up in the centre of the Cornish city in summer 1997, is Dennis Dart/Plaxton Pointer B37F N168KAF, bought new. The company was later taken over by First Group.

Another large independent is Western Greyhound, running services throughout the Duchy and even into Devon. The fleet consists of many modern buses bought new and some second-hand purchases. R478RRA is one of the latter, being an ex-Nottingham City Transport Volvo Olympian/East Lancs. It's seen here in the tiny bus station in St Ives, on 12 June 2010.

The village of Troon, near Camborne, Cornwall, was once home to Grenville Motors. Services were operated into Camborne and beyond, with a small separate operation based near Falmouth. The company also reached Penzance, where I photographed GAL22J in early 1981, on a typical grey day. Formerly 1189 in the Barton fleet, Nottinghamshire, it is a 1971 Bedford YRQ with 52-seat Willowbrook coachwork.

Another company running into Penzance was Harvey's of Mousehole, trading as Blue and Cream. The route was particularly difficult for bus operations, due to the tight corners in the villages en route. Therefore only small vehicles were suitable, such as this Albion Nimbus/ Weymann B31F, seen here in 1977, negotiating the particularly hazardous road layout in Newlyn, the small fishing port just around the bay from Penzance. RJX250 was new to Halifax and has since passed into preservation.